6.5b

You See Me, You Hear Me

A Short Guide to Prayer for Young Adults

FATHER MICHAEL GIESLER

Scepter

Published by Scepter Publishers, Inc.
P.O. Box 1391
New Rochelle, NY 10802
www.scepterpublishers.org

Cover image: shutterstock.com
Cover design and interior layout by
Creative Editorial Solutions

ISBN: 978-1-59417-188-8

Printed in the United States of America

15 14 13 12   1 2 3 4

My Lord and my God, I firmly believe that you are here, that you see me, that you hear me. I adore you with profound reverence. I ask your pardon for my sins and the grace to make this time of prayer fruitful. My Immaculate Mother, St. Joseph my father and lord, my guardian angel, intercede for me.

TABLE OF CONTENTS

PREFACE

"God thirsts that we may thirst for Him"
(St. Augustine, as quoted in CCC, 2560)

What an amazing and consoling state-
ment—to think that the infinite God, who
made all things and sustains all things, deeply
desires that we speak with him and be united
to him. He does not want us to lead a lonely
life, isolated from his goodness and his love.
He wants to communicate with us, and us with
him. Yet how many people today really know
this, or have seriously thought about it?

Maybe you are one of them. Life can get very
busy. There are classes to take, sports to play,
people to see, and a few crises to resolve now
and then. And yes, there is perhaps a whole
world to manage on Facebook and an end-
less barrage of text messages to keep up with.
Though these things are really not so important
or urgent as they seem, society and your friends
keep telling you that they are.

And yet there is something more to life. There's something deep inside each of us that wants to communicate, not only through cyberspace, but in a way that is far more personal and spiritual. We call this special way prayer, and we tap into it with our minds and our hearts. We can know and love—and these two powers make us unlike anything else in the physical universe. In fact, Scripture points to God himself in order to give us a description of what we are like. The Book of Genesis puts it like this: "God created man in his own image, in the image of God He created him; male and female He created them" (Gn 1:27). If we forget that we are made in God's image, with a mind for knowing him and a heart for loving him, we forget the greatest truth about ourselves, and worst of all, we will end up quite unhappy and alone.

Yet we often run from God and from who we really are. Our escape can be into mere activity or busy-ness, or into more harmful things like alcohol, pornography, or drugs. Or we can just fall into time-wasting. And yet we cannot escape the truth about ourselves, and the One for whom we were made. As soon as we understand these deeper realities and act accordingly—our life will have purpose, and we'll find real happiness.

Yes, God is thirsting for you and me, just as he thirsted for water at the well of Sichar, in Samaria, where he stopped after a tiring journey (see Jn 4:1–42). When a certain woman came to the well at midday, he asked her for a drink of water. But he was thirsting even more for her conversion, and as they spoke, he taught her to believe in him, and he changed her life. Let's engage him in conversation. Let's speak to him, and let him speak to us. Like the woman at the well, we too will be amazed at the things he tells us.

Maybe you remember a certain play of Shakespeare from your English course, either in high school or college. It's called *Macbeth,* the story of an ambitious Scottish noble who stopped at nothing, not even murder, to become king. At the end, when his enemies were gathering against him and he saw that his entire kingdom was crumbling, he spoke these famous words: "Life is a tale told by an idiot, full of sound and fury, signifying nothing" (Act V, Scene 5). That is how our life would be if we didn't have God, or if we didn't pay attention to him. But if we develop a life of prayer and virtue, with God's grace, our life will be the opposite of Macbeth's tragic sentence: It will be a tale told by Jesus Christ, full of adventure and love, signifying everything.

This book will help you to find that life. It's about prayer, especially mental prayer, and it explains how a life of prayer will liberate you and give you lasting joy. Not a frivolous, noisy kind of joy which can soon turn bitter, but a deeper, more lasting contentment that will truly sustain you. It will also show how prayer can get you through the toughest moments, when you're tempted to give up or fall into sinful or selfish behavior.

The thoughts in this book are based on Sacred Scripture, the teachings of the Catholic Church, the insights of St. Josemaría Escrivá, founder of Opus Dei, and other great spiritual writers.

I hope you enjoy it and benefit from it.

MENTAL PRAYER: PERSONAL CONVERSATION WITH GOD

What is prayer? Very simply put, prayer is conversation with God. It is communication with the One who made us, through our mind, will, and feelings. It doesn't have to involve mystical visions or special phenomena, though it may. To put it in modern terms, prayer is like an instantaneous wireless connection that costs us nothing. Normally it will involve the practical and personal things of our day—what we're thinking or feeling at each moment—and how they connect with God.

Prayer is above all a dialogue. This term comes from a Greek word that means a conversation between two parties. Prayer is not the same as thinking about something, or introspection, or self-awareness. It is not the same as having feelings inside—such as joy, or anger, or sorrow. Prayer is a true communication where a human person and God interact with one another. It can involve spoken words, as in the case of vocal prayers like the Rosary, or our own interior words, as in the case of mental prayer. As a matter of fact, prayer doesn't have to involve words at all. It can simply be a silent, loving look at one another. We communicate something to God, and he to us.

Prayer is true communication between a person and God.

All of creation is the united work of the three Persons of the Blessed Trinity. This means that the three Persons of the Trinity are everywhere—the Father, the Son, and the Holy Spirit. The Blessed Trinity has created and is sustaining the whole universe. We cannot think a thought, breathe a breath, or have a heartbeat without them. God is closer to us than we are to ourselves. Prayer, therefore, is really the simplest, most immediate thing we can do with God—especially because we are made in his image and likeness, with a mind that can know him, and a will that can love him.

For this reason it doesn't matter what age you are in order to pray. Small children can speak with God (their prayers are often the simplest and best), as long as they are aware of God's existence and that God sees and hears them. When prayer is truly developed, a person has the habit of communicating with God all day long—at work, with her family, during rest. This is obtained by the person's own effort to pray each day, but above all, by God's grace that inspires the person to speak with him.

Our model for prayer as Catholics is Jesus Christ, the Son of God and our Redeemer. By looking at his communication with his Father, we ourselves can learn how to pray effectively. Also, since Christ is God, we can communicate with him directly as well. In fact, we may find our communication with Jesus to be even more natural and effective, since he is a human being like us.

In addition to the Holy Eucharist, which contains Christ himself in his Body and Blood, one of the best places to find Christ is in the Bible. There we will learn the words and attitudes that we need in order to pray well.

FINDING CHRIST
IN SCRIPTURE

Holy Scripture is God's "text message" to us. In these seventy-three books, which the Catholic Church considers divinely inspired, God reveals his truth and love to us. Beginning with the fact of creation, the Bible gives us the history of humanity from its earliest days and the history of God's chosen people. It contains the laws we must follow to be happy, the greatest prayer hymns ever written (the Psalms), and sayings of the prophets and wise men that have instructed millions of people throughout history.

Above all, Scripture contains the words and actions of Jesus Christ, who fulfills the Old Testament and gives us the New Testament—the covenant of his truth and love. If we want to learn how to pray, Christ will give us our first and best lesson.

"And after he had dismissed the crowds, he

went up on the mountain by himself to pray" (Mt 14:23). Though Jesus was God himself, as a human, he felt the need to be alone with his Father. The people had wanted to crown him king after the miracle of the loaves and fishes, but that was not his goal. He did not seek an earthly glory. His human mind and heart needed to converse with God about his real mission: to save souls and to bring as many people as possible to eternal life.

Often we see Jesus withdrawing from the busy-ness and hectic moments of his public life. Though the Gospel doesn't tell us why he does this, we can guess that as a human being, he wanted to be ever closer to his Father God, and to see things always in the light of his Father's will. For this reason he always found the time for personal prayer. For instance, before beginning his very busy and challenging public life, he prayed and fasted for forty days (see Mt 4:1-11). Before choosing his apostles he spent the whole night in prayer (see Lk 6:12). In the Garden of Gethsemani, before his passion and death, he prayed for strength to go forward with God's plan, and he said, "Not as I will, but as thou wilt" (Mt 26:39).

There will be many times in your own life when you will feel the clear need for personal time with God—just he and you. It could be after a strong disappointment, such as failing an important test or losing a good friend. It could also be after a big joy or triumph, such as passing a hard subject, or winning a championship game.

Maybe you're going through a particularly tough time in your soul, such as having doubts about your Faith, or strong temptations against purity. In these moments, you will especially appreciate the power of prayer, where you can speak with Jesus Christ, your greatest friend, who understands you and will never leave you, who himself was tempted severely but in the end said, "Not as I will, but as thou wilt."

Read this stirring text from St. Josemaría in *The Way*. It can wake you up and lead you to what is most important:

> *You seek the friendship of those who, with their conversation and affection, with their company, help you to bear more easily the exile of this world—although sometimes those friends fail you. I don't see anything wrong with that. But*

how is it that you do not seek every day, more eagerly, the company, the conversation of that great friend who will never fail you? " (The Way, *no. 88*).

Prayer in Everyday Things

But Christ did not limit his prayer to tough or demanding moments. Often we see him simply going off alone to a quiet place, leaving his disciples to search for him. One time, upon finding him at prayer, they were so fascinated that they asked him to teach them how to pray. And it was then that he taught them the Our Father, which is the model of prayer for people of all times. If you look carefully at the words, you will conclude that the Our Father doesn't speak so much about extraordinary events or temptations. It is more about ordinary situations... things that we face every day in our lives.

Our Father, who art in heaven, hallowed be thy name. Our existence itself is a gift, and so our everyday life is to give glory to the One who made us, and to praise his name—which, in the Bible, means the person himself.

Thy kingdom come. Every day of our life

should in some way advance God's kingdom on earth, a kingdom of peace, truth, and justice. Though at times it appears only as a mustard seed, it will change the entire world. We can do our part by having faith, hope, and charity, by living a virtuous life, and by offering our work to God.

Thy will be done, on earth as it is in heaven. We exist to carry out God's will in the big and little things of each day. We don't simply want to be resigned to the will of God, we should love it, even if at times it brings disappointment or suffering. In the end, there will always be joy and victory in doing his will.

Give us this day our daily bread. This is the petition part of the Our Father, which is a basic part of all prayer. Our daily bread can certainly mean food, shelter, and the basic necessities of life. It can also mean achieving success at work or school. But above all, our daily bread means the graces and spiritual help that we need to do the will of God each day.

And forgive us our trespasses... Yes, we are sinners and need God's continual forgiveness for our pride, our anger, or other forms of selfishness. Of course, we should go to confession often, but we don't have to wait until then to ask God's pardon.

...as we forgive those who trespass against us. In life there will be people who offend or hurt us, sometimes deliberately, but probably most times without even knowing it. We ask God to give us big hearts that know how to forgive others, and yes, to forget also.

And lead us not into temptation, but deliver us from evil. Since we all have the effects of original sin in us, the result of our first parents' disobedience, we will have to fight against temptation each day—which will come from our selfish desires, and from the evil one.

Amen. In Scripture this word means "So be it," or "Let it be fulfilled." Amen is therefore a fitting way to conclude all kinds of prayer, whether they be adoring God, or thanking him, or making up for sin, or asking for something.

When we look at the words of Christ in the Our Father, and see the way he lived his life—many times breaking out into spontaneous prayer—we can understand why he would tell his disciples to pray always and not to give up (see Lk 18:1). Prayer is not only for emergencies, nor only for Sunday Mass, but for everyday life.

This is the central message of Opus Dei: namely, that God is waiting for us in all the circumstances of our lives. St. Josemaría made this point in a homily called

God is waiting for us in all the circumstances of our lives.

"Passionately Loving the World," which he gave in 1967 at the University of Navarre in Spain:

> *Understand this well: there is something holy, something divine hidden in the most ordinary situations, and it is up to each one of you to discover it.... There is just one life, made of flesh and spirit. And it is this life which has to become, in both soul and body, holy and filled with God. We discover the invisible God in the most visible and material things.*

Your personal conversation with God, sometimes referred to as mental prayer, will help you to discover God in every circumstance of your life. As St. Josemaría used to say, you will learn to turn everything into gold like the legendary King Midas (see *The Forge*, no.742).

Talking With Christ All Day Long

Christ not only teaches us how to pray to his Father God, but he also invites us to speak often with himself throughout the day. "Come to me, all who labor and are heavy laden, and I will give you rest" (Mt 11:28). The New Testament is filled with spontaneous conversations that the apostles had with the Lord.

For instance, we read how John and James first got to know Christ. "Rabbi, where are you staying?" they asked him, and they spent the rest of the day with him (see Jn 2:38–39). Remember also what Jesus said to Nathaniel when he met him for the first time: "Behold, an Israelite indeed, in whom is no guile!" And when Nathaniel asked him how he knew him, Jesus answered, "Before Phillip called you, when you were under the fig tree, I saw you" (Jn 1:47–48).

Jesus has a way of winning people to himself in a most attractive way, and when he speaks to them, he challenges them as well. When Peter, for instance, protested that Jesus was about to wash his feet at the Last Supper, Christ told him, "If I do not wash you, you have no part in me." And Peter, with humility and good humor, answered, "Lord, not my feet only, but also my hands and my head!" (Jn 13:8–9).

Like the apostles, we too should get into the habit of speaking with Christ, his Mother, and the angels and saints at different times during the day. We must not think that prayer is reserved only for church. If we want to live our entire life in union with God, we should desire constant communication—just as many people want to send text messages to their friends all day long, even about the simplest things they are doing. We can do this by means of brief prayers called "aspirations." An aspiration can be as brief as saying "Thank you, Lord" when something good has happened to us, or "Help me, Lord" when we are in trouble. When we're in a crowd of people, such as at school or on a bus, we can pray to God for those around us. If we experience a temptation against faith, we can say with the apostles, "Lord, increase our faith" (Lk 17:5). Or if we are disturbed by impure thoughts or desires, we can say with the leper, "Lord, if you will, you can make me clean" (Lk 5:12) or "Immaculate Heart of Mary, protect me."

Reminders of God are also very helpful. Carrying a crucifix or rosary in your pocket will remind you of who you are: a follower of Christ and a son of Mary. I once heard of a businessman who wanted to remember Christ in the most hectic moments of his day. He not only wanted to feel the crucifix in his pocket, but actually see it on the desk in front of him, especially in his most stressful moments. But he couldn't actually place the cross or the rosary on the desk, or else people would think it strange. So he simply fashioned two paper clips together in the form of a cross—near the phone, which was always ringing. Whenever he saw that paper-clip cross, he would say a little prayer and offer his work to God.

Perhaps you could come up with something similar—so that you always remember what your life is about and where you are going. There's an important reason for this. If we don't find God during our day, it is very easy to fall into a kind of monologue with ourselves. We would become immersed in our own world of excitement and enthusiasms. But they would not last, because they're based on our own passing desires and often end up in disappointment and boredom, or in different kinds of fear, anger, or sadness. But prayer is a dialogue that really liberates us from ourselves. Saying short prayers and aspirations is like opening a window for fresh air in a stuffy room, or like opening the curtains to let the sunshine in.

Prayer from the Heart

"These people honor me with their lips, but their hearts are far from me" (Is 29:13). God asked his chosen people for personal faithfulness; he wanted more than external sacrifices. He wanted their true attention and affection in the things that they did. He wanted them to communicate their fears, their sorrows, and their joys to him. This is truly prayer from the heart, not simply a mindless repetition of certain words or phrases. In other words, he wanted a true dialogue—not a monologue, as we just saw.

We value this in people. When you speak with a friend, you really want to know his authentic thoughts and desires about something. You also hope that he is really listening to you, not absorbed by his own ideas only. If the person is a real friend, he or she might even share with you the reasons for important decisions in his or her life. Personal prayer is like that; it is conversation with our great Friend, who will never fail us and who wants to know what is in our heart—that is, our true motivation.

The Catechism has a marvelous description of what the heart means in prayer and in the Bible. It is worth quoting at length:

> *The heart is the dwelling place where I am, where I live; according to the Semitic or Biblical expression, the heart is the place 'to which I withdraw.' The heart is our hidden center, beyond the grasp of our reason and of others; only the Spirit of God can fathom the human heart and know it fully. The heart is the place of decision, deeper than our psychic drives. It is the place of truth, where we choose life or death (CCC, 2563).*

Quite often we act in ways that are far from the real us. It's easy to escape into pleasures, curiosities, and technologies that distract us from our true selves. They can fill up our time, but they do not teach us anything about ourselves, nor help us to become better or wiser persons. But prayer and reflection give us depth. Through daily prayer we always remember who we are and where we're going.

If our heart—the place of our decisions—is for God we will value the time of prayer. We will want our life to be a true conversation with God, not a boring chat with ourselves. We will value the time

> *Prayer and reflection give us depth. Through daily prayer we always remember who we are and where we're going.*

that we have set aside for a heart-to-heart conversation with God.

The Benefits of Regular Prayer

Do you like to climb hills or mountains? There are two clear advantages in climbing: apart from the opportunity for exercise, which is always good, there is also the opportunity for wonderful views. A good hill of 500 feet altitude or more can give you a sweeping view of your neighborhood, of the sky, of where you've come from, and possibly where you're going. Such is also the benefit of a regular time for prayer. Talking to God is like climbing a high hill, or part of a mountain, to come closer to God and to see things better. As you reflect more about your family, your work, your friendships—and your troubles, too—you gain perspective. You see that some things in your life are rather silly and should be forgotten, while others are more important and should receive your attention.

For instance, I know of a young woman who was constantly worried about how she looked. She was always comparing herself with other girls in her class in terms of appearance, studies, boyfriends—and she was often uncertain and agitated about where she stood. But one day, during her time of prayer, the Holy Spirit helped her to see something new: how she related to her own family. And she realized that, while she was obsessing about being popular with her friends, she had grown to be unkind to her mother, quite distant from her father, and had come to see her little brother only as an annoyance. In other words, because she prayed, she began to see things differently.

Another benefit of mental prayer, besides gaining perspective, is to ask God for help.

Most people, when they hear the word prayer, think that asking for God's help is its main purpose. And certainly all of us have plenty of things to pray for each day. You can ask God's help in getting a certain assignment finished, or in understanding someone in your class; or you can beg God's assistance if you're being tempted, and feel quite weak, by certain sites on the Internet or something else. Prayer gives you extra strength to do the things you must and avoid the things that are harmful. That makes perfect sense, since prayer is really companionship. Instead of facing life alone, you're facing it with someone else: Jesus Christ and his grace.

When you pray consistently, you not only gain a balanced perspective, you become calmer about things. Our Lord said as much in the Sermon on the Mount: "Do not be anxious for your life…but seek first his kingdom and his righteousness, and all these things shall be yours as well" (Mt 6:25, 33). So often you can worry about things like money, health, food, and clothing. Of course you need these things, but you can exaggerate their importance and even become obsessed about them. Your mind becomes clearer because of the time spent with God, and you are able to overcome feelings or emotions which can suddenly spring upon you like a thunderstorm: anger, fear, sadness, even an insistent craving for something harmful or silly. Conversation with God helps you to see all these things for what they are, or for what they are not.

There is an old story about an Indian and his son. Apparently a horse had escaped from the village, and the chief told his twelve-year-old son to go into the hills, find it, and bring it back. The boy, enthused that his father had entrusted him with such an important task, and looking forward to the adventure of pursuit, was about to leave the village with only a rope in his hand to tie the horse. But his father asked, "Son, why do you not bring food and water with you?"

The boy answered, "Without food and water I run faster, Father." But the wise chief answered him, "You may run faster, son, but you will not run far." Obviously it takes a lot more to retrieve a runaway stallion than the boy had bargained for.

Regular prayer, along with the Holy Eucharist, is the bread that sustains you in your journey through life. It provides sustenance for all the circumstances of your day, whether expected or unexpected.

Spiritual Reading

> *"Don't neglect your spiritual reading. Reading has made many saints"* (The Way, no. 116).

> *"By reading," you wrote me, "I build up a store of fuel. It seems a lifeless pile, but I often find that my mind spontaneously draws from it material which fills my prayer with life and inflames my thanksgiving after communion"* (The Way, no. 117).

Good spiritual reading puts us in touch with the saints and great writers of the Church throughout the centuries. It is true that prayer should be something personal and unique, but it draws much greater depth and power from the communion of saints—that is, the immense spiritual treasury of people who have prayed throughout the centuries and left us a testimony of their spiritual life. If we have common sense, we will realize that our own experience, by itself, is not enough to pray well over the long run. Christ's Church is called the Mystical Body, which means that somehow we are all inserted into that body. We are not isolated from one another, and we can help each other to pray. Even people from past centuries can help us to pray better.

For instance, the works of St. Teresa of Avila and St. John of the Cross, who lived in the sixteenth century can be of great help. Their writings describe the path of the soul to God and the different stages through which it must pass.

First, they explain that there will be a stage of purification, when we struggle to avoid sin and need to make many acts of contrition; then there will be a stage of advancement, in which we grow especially in the virtues of faith, hope, and charity.

Finally, there is the stage of union or perfection, in which almost all of our thoughts and desires are united to Christ. In this kind of prayer—also called infused contemplation—we ourselves do not have to speak, for it is God himself who speaks to us and loves us. This kind of prayer is the closest thing to heaven that we can experience on earth.

Great spiritual books can also give you insights into the nature of the Church and her sacraments and how you can participate in them more effectively. They help you to understand human nature, both in its positive and negative aspects, and how to overcome sin in your life. *The Confessions of Saint Augustine,* for instance, has provided powerful spiritual reading for people throughout the centuries, since it describes how this famous bishop and theologian of the early Church found God at last, after many years of wandering.

The writings of St. Josemaría, whom Bl. Pope John Paul II called the "saint of ordinary life," give practical advice and encouragement for finding God in daily life and becoming a saint through the grace of our baptismal calling. They are filled with inspiring yet practical ways on how to lead a deep life of prayer every day, especially in connecting our work with Jesus in those hidden years of his ordinary work in Nazareth.

Among these writings are the trilogy of *The Way, The Furrow,* and *The Forge*—which provide short and incisive points that will ignite your prayer—and longer works such as *Christ Is Passing By* and *Friends of God.*

Then, of course, there are many excellent descriptions and commentaries on the Bible that will help you to understand and apply Scripture to your own life. The Navarre Bible, with its introductions and footnotes for each sacred book, is a good example. It will help you to understand the origin and meaning of the books of the Old and New Testaments. The writings of the Bible were written by the Holy Spirit himself through the words of a human author; its verses therefore contain a message for all times and peoples.

A good biblical commentary will give you both the text and the context of biblical passages, and how they have been interpreted by the Church throughout the centuries. Before reading the sacred text, by the way, always be sure to say a prayer to the Holy Spirit so that you can really grasp its meaning and apply it to your daily life.

If you want your conversation with God to have direction and purpose, therefore, good readings are indispensable. When your own mind and experience fails, the mind and experiences of others can give you more insight and energy to speak with God; in this way you will see what is truly advantageous for your journey on this earth.

Plan to Pray

You might think that prayer should always be spontaneous—to be done in times of great emotion, danger, or need. To make a plan of prayer somehow seems unnecessary, and perhaps even a bit phony. Why should I force myself to pray? Why should I subject myself to a schedule? How can I, as free person, get anything out that?

It reminds me of that challenging little point in *The Way*, where St. Josemaría points to the real reason for contact with God:

> *"You told me that to tie yourself to a plan of life, to a schedule, would be so monotonous! And I answered, 'It is monotonous because you lack Love'" (The Way, no.77).*

If we truly realized who we are as God's children, we would not wait until an emergency situation in order to pray. It is precisely because we are made in God's image and likeness that we should desire to pray every day.

Furthermore, if we always wait until we feel like praying or are "in the mood" for it, we may be worshiping ourselves, and not God. Rather than God being a loving Father with whom we want to communicate, he simply becomes a last resort for our unhappiness.

However, if we look at our day carefully, and realize that the most important thing we can do each day is to grow closer to God, we will indeed find time for prayer. And we will plan ahead so that we can be with him.

As St. Josemaría says in the above point, the test of true prayer is love. When you love someone, don't you want to be with him or her regularly, and make all kinds of sacrifices to do so? Don't you owe at least that much to the One who created you and saved you from sin?

At times it may take some creativity to pray when you're at home. There may be distractions like television or video games, or siblings. Little brothers and sisters are great—you should love them very much—but they probably won't ever realize you are trying to pray. So you'll have to be clever when you're at home. If you have your own room, that's a great advantage. You can just close your door and speak with your heavenly Father, who sees everything. But if you don't have such privacy, you may have to go out for a walk, or go to the basement and spend time praying there.

If you are in a college dorm or residence, it will be harder to get to bed early enough in order to wake up for prayer in the morning. You obviously

The test of true prayer is love.

can't force others, who may go to bed at a later hour, to follow *your* schedule.

If you have your own bedroom, it will be easier to make your own schedule. At times you may have to postpone your prayer until later in the day. But no matter what, you can be sure that God appreciates your effort to give him your time.

The best plan is simply to spend more time at your parish church, at an adoration chapel, or some other place to pray. There you should have plenty of time to do your reading and mental prayer in a quiet, undistracted setting.

Whatever you decide, be sure that God will be pleased with your sacrifice and your effort to find time for him each day—whether you're at home or away from home.

A good plan of prayer will contain the following each day:

A specific time to get up and to make a morning offering. It might be hard—even heroic—to get up in the morning sometimes. But this too is part of your love for God. You begin your day by overcoming sleepiness and giving your time and attention to God. Your morning offering can take many forms, but I suggest that it be something like this: "O my Lord, I offer you all my prayers, works, joys, and sufferings in union with your Most Sacred Heart and the Holy Sacrifice of the Mass." This focuses you on God and his glory from the first moment of your day.

A time for personal prayer. This book is mostly about mental prayer, which is essential for keeping in personal contact with God. You might try to do at least fifteen minutes a day of personal conversation in a quiet, recollected place. Eventually you can build up to a half-hour or more.

Of course, the best place is before the Holy Eucharist, in a church or adoration chapel. But good prayer can also be done in your room or in a quiet place where you can focus your thoughts and speak with God.

Above all, remember that mental prayer is a consequence of Love, with a capital L. Christ is our greatest friend; we would not think of spending our day without some time to be with him.

Holy Mass and Communion. The greatest prayer of all is Jesus' own prayer at the Sacrifice of the Mass, where he offers himself to the Father in the love of the Holy Spirit. The Mass is the re-actualization of what Christ did at the Last Supper and on the Cross. It is really the ultimate prayer, since it contains within itself all the different forms of prayer in an infinite and perfect way: adoration, petition, reparation, and thanksgiving. Jesus Christ offered all four kinds of prayer at the Last Supper and on Calvary. Each time you go to Mass, therefore, you are connecting yourself to the greatest prayer of all, which makes your own prayer even more valuable, since it draws power and energy from Christ's own sacrifice.

The Mass is truly "where the action is;" it unites us with the angels and saints, the souls in purgatory, and all of our brothers and sisters in the Church on earth. We are never alone at the Mass; through the sacrifice of Christ we are united to men and women of all times, and especially with our fellow Catholics who are participating in the Mass with us. The action of the Holy Spirit expands our minds and hearts, as we offer our specific intentions during the Eucharistic Prayer: for our family and friends, for the good of the country, for our vocation.

The moment of receiving Holy Communion is a most precious and intimate time with God. It is your chance to speak directly and personally with Christ, the One who has given himself to you in his Body and Blood. Since it is his risen body, he brings all of paradise with him: God the Father and God the Holy Spirit, his mother Mary, and all the angels and saints.

But despite your best intentions, you may not always feel close to God when you receive Holy Communion. If no thoughts or affections come to you in those moments, you might recall some ideas that St. Josemaría offered from his own thanksgiving after Communion. After Mass, when Jesus was still present inside of him, he would recall the following. First,

Christ is our king, and we want him to rule in our hearts with his kingdom of peace, joy, and justice. He is also our physician, and he wants to heal us; so let us reveal ourselves to him completely—our worries, our anger, our fears, and our faults. He is our teacher, and we can ask him to explain things we don't understand, and how to live our lives for him. Above all, he is our greatest and truest friend, and we should go to him with complete confidence.

Here is St. Josemaría's description of how Christ indeed is our greatest friend:

> *"He calls us his friends; and he is the one who took the first step, because he loved us first. Still, he does not impose his love—he offers it.... If he sees us cold, unwilling, rigid perhaps with the stiffness of a dying interior life, his tears will be our life—'I say to you, my friend, arise and walk,' (see Jn 11:43) leave that narrow life which is no life at all"* (Christ Is Passing By, *no. 93).*

Always Time for Mary

Our daily plan should always include some

time with Mary, the Mother of God. Perhaps we could spend some moments of our mental prayer speaking to her personally and asking her for things. She will always be there, listening to us with her Son and the other Persons of the Trinity.

We can ask her for so many things: for greater charity and humility, for purity of heart and mind, for the needs of our families and friends. Our conversation can be very simple and direct, like a small child with his or her mother. She can read our hearts, and already knows our needs better than we do. So we should be very confident in praying to her each day.

One of her favorite prayers is the holy Rosary, since it contains the words that the angel Gabriel spoke to her on the day that she became the mother of God: "Hail, full of grace, the Lord is with you" (Lk 1:28). Since she loves to hear those words again and again, we shouldn't mind repeating them fifty or a hundred times! We know that even if we become distracted at times, she never gets distracted, and she is most pleased that we are making the sacrifice to pay attention to her—like a young man singing a serenade to his sweetheart. His mind may wander at times, but his heart is with his beloved, and she knows that he is singing to please her and only her.

The Rosary is also a powerful contemplative prayer. Our life becomes immersed in the events of Mary's own life and those of her Son, as we consider each mystery of the Rosary: joyful, sorrowful, luminous, or glorious. Have you ever had family gatherings in which your parents or grandparents reminisced about past events and people in their lives? Didn't the sharing of those memories bring everyone together much more? Funny things and sad things, good things and tough things—they are all part of your family history and you feel close to each other in sharing them.

A similar thing happens when praying the Rosary. As we "reminisce" about the lives of Jesus and Mary, our own lives become more united with those of Our Lady and her Son. In a way, we actually begin to live the mysteries of Mary's life: the joy of the annunciation and the visitation, the sorrow of the crucifixion, the wonder of the miracle of Cana, the glory of the assumption as Mary is triumphantly received into heaven by God and his angels.

Finally, the Rosary is a great prayer of petition. Not only can we ask the Mother of God for personal things, but talk to her about big world problems that seem so hard to solve: peace among nations, the protection of unborn children, the health of the family.

Let us not forget that Mary crushes the devil's head under her immaculate heel, since she was conceived without sin. And because she is so close to God—the daughter of God the Father, the Mother of God the Son, the Spouse of God the Holy Spirit—she is truly all powerful in her petition. We can always be confident if we go to her in the Rosary and other vocal prayers that she loves, such as the Memorare, the Hail Holy Queen, and the Regina Coeli.

Our daily plan should always include some time with Mary. She will always be there, listening to us with her Son.

There are many other spiritual practices that you can incorporate into your plan of life. It is very helpful, for instance, to include a brief examination of conscience in the evening. It's simple and takes just a few minutes. First, review your day in the presence of God and take note of things that went well or did not go well. Then give thanks or make an act of contrition to God with a good resolution for the next day.

Also, be sure to go regularly to the great sacrament of confession, which gives such grace and peace; there you will find Christ the Good Shepherd who always forgives you when you confess your sins humbly and sincerely.

Besides these spiritual practices, keep in mind that prayer can also be spontaneous, for the Holy Spirit is like the wind and works in mysterious and unexpected ways during the day. He can give us many inspirations and move us with his gifts at any time. But he will be more likely to act within you if you have been generous with your time during the day and make plans to speak with him.

Qualities of Good Prayer

Sincerity One of the most important qualities of good prayer is sincerity. We should never have any secrets from God—it would be absurd to try! Our conversation should be about what is really going on in our lives, as far as we can see. We should speak to him about good things and bad things, what went well, and what did not go so well. We should speak about big issues and ideals, and also the little frustrations of our day. If we are children of God, we can even get away with complaining once in a while, as St. Teresa of Avila did one day when a cart holding her convent's goods overturned in the mud. Frustrated, she told God, "If that's the way you treat your friends, no wonder you have so few of them!" I'm sure that God smiled on her as she picked herself out of the mud. He will smile on us, too, if we pray with sincerity like St. Teresa.

Faith We must also pray with faith and the firm conviction that God can truly grant our petition. Christ often chastised his apostles because of their little faith. They were always thinking humanly…they did not trust Christ's power to protect or save them. For example, when Christ told Peter to walk across the water, he couldn't do it, because he was thinking too much in human terms. The Gospel tells us that he became frightened by the wind (see Mt 14:30); he let that external thing undermine his trust in Christ, who was actually giving him the power to walk upon the water at that moment. When we pray, we should have the absolute conviction that God indeed hears us and has the love and power to help us.

Perseverance   Good prayer is persevering. "Ask, and it will be given to you; seek, and you will find; knock, and it will be opened to you" (Lk 11:9). Christ encourages us to not give up in our prayers. In another text he even compares God to an unjust judge who will not listen to a widow's lawsuit, but finally she wears him out by her insistence (see Lk 18:1–8). If the widow got what she wanted through her persistence, we can be even more confident that God will listen to our prayers. But we should not give up if we do not get results right away. If our intention is good, and we are not asking for something wrong or sinful, we will surely win God's favor in the end.

But let's be aware of something that can also be disconcerting about prayer. Often God appears to ignore our petition, instead giving us something we didn't ask for, which in the end is much better for us.

I remember the story of the boy who asked for a bicycle. He kept asking God and his parents for a bike, but he didn't receive one. Instead, God gave him a much greater gift: a little sister. The time that he would have spent on his bike now became time to help his mother care for his little sister. And eventually, God was so good that he also gave him a bike so that he could go to the store to buy things that his mother couldn't. But God first made him wait for the bike. This is often the way God works. He doesn't give us what we ask for right away, but gives us something better, though we may not appreciate it at the time. The main point is that we should persevere in our prayer; no effort is ever wasted.

Humility Good prayer is humble. The proud person doesn't see the need to pray; he thinks that he has everything under control, or that he can get all that he needs by his own efforts. But the humble person knows that his whole life is a gift, and that he needs everything from God. He also knows that he has no right to demand things from God. He presents his petitions, but in the end, he lets God decide. And when he prays, he doesn't give God a list of his accomplishments, like the pharisee in the Gospel parable (see Lk 18:9-14). He simply recognizes that he is a sinner and asks for God's mercy.

Forgiveness God doesn't like hypocrites who ask him for things but are not willing to give the same things to others. This includes forgiveness. If we want God to hear our prayers, we cannot hold a grudge against anyone. If someone has offended us, we should forgive him from the bottom of our heart and then speak to God in prayer.

If we find it difficult to forgive someone, we can ask God to help us. We should also ask forgiveness from someone that we ourselves have offended. Christ said as much in Matthew 5:23: "So if you are offering your gift at the altar, and there remember that your brother has something against you, leave your gift there before the altar and go; first be reconciled to your brother, and then come and offer your gift."

The Four Great Kinds of Prayer

Catholic theologians over the centuries have taught that there are four great kinds of prayer that reflect what Christ did throughout his life, particularly on the cross and at Holy Mass. They are *adoration, petition, thanksgiving,* and *atonement.* In some way, our most personal and spontaneous kinds of prayer fit into one of these four types, even though our words and thoughts can vary a great deal.

Adoration Adoration is our recognition that God is number one in our lives. This is difficult for our modern mentality, which is so independent and admires science, technology, art, and other human accomplishments but easily forgets the source of all these things. God alone should we adore. If we simply open our eyes, we can see God's power and greatness in the mountains and stars, and the beauty of the universe. We see that God can draw good out of very tough circumstances, and that he is the cause of all things. As he revealed to Moses, his sacred name is "I Am" (Ex 3:14): God is the One who is. All other beings receive their existence from him. He is the source of all goodness; even our most personal experiences reflect his goodness.

Petition Petition is what most people have in mind when they think of prayer. It means asking God for something. Since we really are in need of many things, our personal prayer will naturally have a lot of this. We can ask him for success in our studies, for good friendships, for health if we are sick, for clarity of mind if we are confused. It is also good to ask him for things that are beyond our own self-interest. We should pray regularly—as the Holy Father does—for world peace, for the protection of the family, and for innocent human life. We should also pray for vocations to the Church and her holy institutions, since they give glory to God and do immense good for others. We particularly pray for those who are sick or in need and for those who are deceased—that they will go to God as soon as possible, and enjoy eternal life.

Reparation Reparation is the most difficult kind of prayer and often the most forgotten. But it is extremely important. It is the prayer of Jesus on the cross when he said, "Father, forgive them; for they know not what they do" (Lk 23:34). He made up for sin by his prayer and suffering at that moment.

By offering himself as a victim, he restored his executioners, and indeed, the whole human race, to unity with his Father. In a word, he "repaired" what had been broken by sin and atoned for the willful rebellion of men and women against God and his loving plan for them. Bl. Pope John Paul II explained this whole mystery in terms of Christ's human heart:

> *"The redemption of the world—this tremendous mystery of love in which creation is renewed—is, at its deepest root, the fullness of justice in a human heart— the heart of the first-born son, in order that it may become justice in the hearts of many human beings..."* (Redeemer of Man, no. 9).

Acts of reparation can be made many times during the day: when you pass by a movie theater where they're showing bad films, or a hospital or clinic where they perform abortions, when you hear somebody cursing or attacking the Church, when you see some scandalous event featured in the newspaper.

These are crucial moments to make acts of reparation, and, as the word "crucial" means, unite your prayer with Christ on the cross in order to redeem the human race and atone for sins, both our own and those of others. "Lord, have mercy," "Father, forgive them," and "Most Sacred Heart of Jesus, have pity on us" are all examples of brief aspirations that you could say at these times.

Thanksgiving Thanksgiving flows from a grateful heart. The more we see God's love for us and the workings of his providence in our lives and that of others, the more we will desire to give thanks. Again, this was Jesus' prayer at the Last Supper and at every Mass; Eucharist actually comes from the Greek word for thanksgiving. As he broke the bread, Christ gave thanks for his Father's love and forgiveness pouring forth on the human race. He was thankful for his apostles and their vocation and for the Church that he was founding.

We too can give thanks for all of these

things, along with personal favors that God has given to us in school or work, with our family and our friends. The more we pray, the more we will recognize all the ways that we should give thanks to God for his benefits. As Psalm 23 says, he is truly the Good Shepherd who leads us to green pastures and fountains of pure water, and he protects us always if we should walk "in the valley of death."

The more you see God's love for you and his providence in your life, the more you will desire to give thanks.

Meditation and Other Forms of Prayer

As we said above, all prayers in some way can fit into adoration, petition, atonement, and thanksgiving. But as far as the format or content of mental prayer goes, St. Josemaría never gave any specific recommendation. He liked to stress personal conversation above all else—which consists both in speaking and listening to God. In *The Way* he describes prayer in the most elemental manner:

> *"You don't know how to pray? Put your-
> self in the presence of God, and as soon
> as you have said, 'Lord, I don't know how
> to pray!' you can be sure you've already
> begun" (no. 90).*

However, even though prayer will always be
a personal communication with God and will
in many ways depend upon a person's temperament and background, there are certain
kinds of prayer used throughout the ages by
the saints. You should know about them, and
perhaps try one or two of them to see if they
work for you.

Meditative Prayer The first type is called
meditative prayer. Take a text from Scripture
or a good spiritual reading book, read it carefully, try to understand it well, then apply it to
your own life, speaking with God about it. It
could be an entire passage or just one phrase.
If you're using the Gospel, it could be a teach-
ing from Christ's sermon on the mount or one
of his miracles...for instance, when the leper
says, "Lord, if you will, you can make me clean"
(Lk 5:12). This could be an excellent meditative prayer if you are experiencing any kind of

temptation—such as against faith or purity. It is a prayer of humility and urgent petition.

Another great text, which St. Josemaría liked to use often, was from St. Paul: "We know that in everything God works for good with those who love him" (Rom 8:28). This is an encouraging passage to consider if you are going through an illness or a misunderstanding, or if you feel frustrated about something.

At other times your meditation could be from reading a good spiritual book, or one of the Psalms. These prayer hymns, composed centuries ago, contain all the vividness of life itself, with its sorrows, anguish, joys, and triumphs. They are a marvelous summary of how the human mind and heart communicate with their Creator: with praise, thanksgiving, petition, and penance. As we mentioned above, Psalm 23 is an all-time favorite of many people, both young and old: "The Lord is my shepherd. I shall not want.... Even though I walk through the valley of the shadow of death, I fear no evil" (Ps 23:1, 4).

Many people develop the custom of writing down in their notebook, or using their electronic device to jot down, different ideas that come to them during the day. It could be something that they've read or thought about, or an experience that they have had.

These ideas will often be from the Holy Spirit himself. They are insights that you can use later in your mental prayer—to go more deeply into them, or to draw some conclusion from them. St. Josemaría for many years would write down these inspirations in what he called his "Catalina" notes—in honor of St. Catherine of Siena. Those notes helped him in his daily prayer, and many of them came to be included in his later books. Such a system may also be very helpful to you in your prayer life.

Conversational Prayer Another type of prayer is spontaneous, free-flowing conversation with God, taken from your everyday experiences. For instance, one day you may wish to pray for or about your family. You can ask God how you can love them more, and how they can find more happiness in their lives. Another time, you may wish to ask for help in your studies or for the grace to grow in some good character trait you want to acquire. This type of prayer has the fluidity of life itself and is very natural, as St. Josemaría put it in *The Way*:

> *"You wrote to me: 'To pray is to talk with God. But about what?' About what? About him, and yourself: joys, sorrows, successes and failures, great ambitions, daily worries—even your weaknesses! And acts of thanksgiving and petition— and love and reparation. In short, to get to know him and get to know yourself— 'to get acquainted!'" (no. 91).*

Aspirations As mentioned earlier, aspirations are quick prayers that can be said throughout the day. They consist of short phrases like "Hail full of grace," "Jesus, I love you," "Lord help me," or a prayer to another person in heaven such as St. Joseph or St. Nicholas. We can literally say thousands of aspirations as we walk down the street or walk up and down the stairs. They keep us in the presence of God and prevent us from thinking about ourselves too much: our fears, our anger, our sadness. These short prayers keep us thinking of God, so that our life little by little becomes a dialogue of love.

Vocal Prayers Vocal prayers—prayers with a set formula of words—have a special value when they are drawn from the Word of God himself, or from the liturgy of the Church, or from the writings of great saints throughout the centuries. The fact that vocal prayers always use the same words, such as the Our Father and Glory Be, does not mean that they are boring or monotonous. If we say those words with attention, they help our souls immensely because they come from a divine source. They literally help us to think as Christ and the greatest saints thought.

The words of the Rosary, for instance, have been said by the greatest men and women saints in the Church for the last thousand years. And of course they were first pronounced by the Angel Gabriel to the Mother of God, and recorded by St. Luke in his Gospel.

It may be helpful at times to take the vocal prayers of the Mass to your mental prayer; there you will discover their depth and beauty, and you will say them with greater attention and devotion.

But even if you get distracted while saying

Vocal prayers help our souls immensely because they come from a divine source.

vocal prayers—whether alone or with others—you shouldn't worry but simply keep returning your attention to them, once and again. You can be sure that God and his Mother will be greatly pleased at your efforts.

Contemplation The highest kind of prayer is called contemplation, which can take place either in mental or vocal prayer. In contemplation we experience a great peace and joy inside of ourselves, a joy that no experience on earth can give. We have the conviction that we are just there with God, and he is the One who speaks. This highest kind of prayer is more affective than meditative, because Love has literally possessed our souls, and we see and desire and feel everything in terms of God's love. It is also called infused contemplation, because it does not come through our own efforts but from the Holy Spirit who produces it within us. Usually this prayer of perfect love and union with God comes after years of prayer and sacrifice and often after a long period of trial and spiritual darkness where a person can even feel very far from God. However, God can also favor a beginner with this kind of prayer because his goodness and mercy are without bounds.

OTHER TIPS FOR
GOOD PRAYER

St. Josemaría never liked to give any fixed method for praying. He preferred to encourage personal conversation with God, which could change according to the needs and circumstances of life. He did emphasize complete sincerity with God always, talking to him one-on-one and not remaining anonymous. Even if nothing comes to us in our mental prayer, he counseled patience and perseverance.

When to Pray

Of course, a person can pray at any time, in any place. Since God is omnipresent, and since we're made in his image and likeness, we can always direct our thoughts and desires to him. We could be walking down the street, preparing to work, going to sleep, or playing a sport. But it does help to have a fixed time for longer conversations with God. These times will be like the heat or radiation source of prayer for the entire day.

How long should your mental prayer be? The best thing is to check with your spiritual director—usually a priest—or some experienced person with whom you can speak about your spiritual life. He may ask you to begin with a certain amount of mental prayer each day and gradually increase the time as you grow closer to God. Except on retreats, your prayer need not be too long, because you obviously have things to do, and you want to sanctify your day and the duties that God has given to you. But in general, if you can give God at least twenty minutes of your undivided attention each day, you are off to a good start. Eventually, I recommend that you reach the goal of doing a half hour in the morning and a half hour in the evening. This will give a good balance to your day and supply you with the spiritual fuel and energy that you need for all of your activity.

Be sure to pray at a time when you are alert. It's difficult to pray late at night, or when you're very tired, since you can fall asleep. The best time is when you're fully alert, so you give God "prime time," so to speak. This could be in the early morning before Mass or breakfast or right after a cup of coffee; or it could be in the late afternoon or early evening.

Where to Pray

The best places for prayer are quiet and without distractions. The most appropriate place, of course, will be a chapel or church where the Blessed Sacrament is present. There you can speak with Christ directly—in his body, blood, soul, and divinity. But you can also pray in your room, looking at a crucifix or a picture of Mary—or with a good book. If it is quiet, a walk in the park could also be an appropriate place to do your mental prayer; the things of nature, which God made, can help you to pray with adoration and thanksgiving.

Your posture should be attentive. At times you may wish to be on your knees in order to express greater reverence and attentiveness. When sitting, avoid a sofa or chair that is too soft or comfortable, since you could doze off or become distracted. The best type of chair will be moderately hard—like the pew in a church or chapel—but not uncomfortable. Also, while praying, it is better to avoid a crouching position. It is best to sit up straight, with eyes toward the tabernacle or the cross, or closed in meditation (unless you're sleepy!).

Opening and Closing Prayers

In order to focus better, you may like to use an introductory prayer that focuses your mind and puts you in the presence of God. For example, the prayer at the beginning of this book can help:

> *"My Lord and my God, I firmly believe that you are here, that you see me, that you hear me. I adore you with profound reverence. I ask your pardon for my sins and the grace to make this time of prayer fruitful. My Immaculate Mother, St. Joseph my father and lord, my guardian angel, intercede for me."*

Just by saying these words attentively you are already praying. Notice that it begins with a clear awareness of God's presence. We don't daydream or think about things by ourselves, like a kind of monologue. We truly believe that we speak to God and that he listens to us. He knows us better than we know ourselves, but he wants to hear from us. We continue with an act of adoration and recognize that the purpose of our life is to give God glory, since all we have is a gift from him. We also ask pardon for our sins, since our faults of pride, laziness, or sensuality separate us from him.

On our own we cannot pray well. For this reason we ask God for the grace to speak and to listen to him; this is not a monologue but a true conversation. To help us pray we also ask for the intercession of experts in prayer: Mary, who spoke with Christ as a child and a man and continues in loving conversation with him forever in heaven; St. Joseph, the head of the Holy Family, who lived and prayed with Christ and taught him how to work; and our guardian angel, whose mission is precisely to help us pray well and get to heaven when we die. Our angel can cleanse our imagination and memory to help us avoid distractions, and he can give us strength to resist the attacks of the evil one, who does not want us to pray.

At the end of our prayer, we can say: "I thank you, my God, for the good resolutions, affections, and inspirations that you have communicated to me in this time of prayer. I ask your help in putting them into effect. My Immaculate Mother, St. Joseph my father and lord, my guardian angel, intercede for me."

Resolutions, Affections, and Inspirations

Good prayer will engage all the powers of our souls: to consider and to know a truth, using our memory, imagination, and intellect; to will or desire something; to express emotions such as joy, sadness, fear, and love. When we pray well, all three of these powers are activated. We find that our minds, wills, and emotions are elevated and purified by contact with God. Good prayer, then, will have resolutions for our will, affections for our emotions, and feelings, and inspirations for our mind.

Resolutions in prayer could include the determination to get up on time in the morning, to be kind to someone that we find annoying, to do our work more conscientiously, or to pay a visit to someone who is sick. These resolutions strengthen and perfect our will to act as Christ and his saints would act.

Affections in prayer include sharing joys and successes with God—such as victory in a sport, a good grade, a strong friendship. They can also include sufferings, uncertainty, and disappointment.

Inspirations in prayer are ideas or insights that God gives to us. For instance, we can understand better the mystery of the Trinity and how we can truly speak with God the Father, God the Son, and God the Holy

Your mind, will, and emotions are elevated by contact with God.

Spirit. We can grasp better the meaning of one of the sacraments, or a point from the Catechism that we did not understand. We might receive an insight into a situation of ordinary life: for instance, how to set better priorities in our work or how to understand a difficult person.

Not every prayer will have all three of them. It is good to keep in mind that we are all different. Those who are more inclined to ideas will probably have more inspirations in their prayer because that is the way that God made them and communicates to them. Those who are more inclined to action will probably have more resolutions—for their work, their family, and their friends. Those who are more sensitive to their emotions may have a more affective prayer, with feelings of joy or sorrow. But no matter what your temperament, it is good to ask God to give you all three of them. The intellectual person often needs more action and feelings; the active person needs more ideals and sensitivity; the emotional person needs more reasons and firm resolutions of the will.

Nonetheless, you shouldn't feel bad if you don't have all three in a given time of prayer. God is still pleased that you choose to spend time with him—out of love for him—even if you "don't get anything out of it." At times, you may be content to repose in God's presence and experience the meaning of Christ's words: "Come to me all you who labor and are heavy laden, and I will give you rest" (Mt 11:28). This is a most beautiful and simple kind of prayer, and we should not force ourselves to go beyond it.

Of course, when we finish our prayer, we should always give thanks to God for the resolutions, affections, and inspirations that we did receive. Most of the time, they will all come from God, though we have to do our part to bring them about. At the end of this little book I will give some examples of different types of prayer that can help you to do this.

OBSTACLES TO
MENTAL PRAYER

Though prayer is a wonderful and necessary practice in our life, there can be obstacles to doing it. Some come from people and things around us, but most come from ourselves. By clearly identifying these obstacles, we can counteract them and go forward with wisdom and confidence, coming ever closer to God.

One clear obstacle is what we call activism, which is measuring life in terms of adrenaline and action. We tend to be quite busy in our country. There are miles to travel, exams to take, friends to meet, and sports to play. None of these are bad things, but they can take us away from the real meaning of our life, which can only be discovered through personal prayer. Let's avoid that activist frame of mind, which says, "I'm so busy—how can I fit in prayer?" We have to convince ourselves that prayer is not a waste of time or a boring activity. It really gives depth and vitality to our life.

Another danger to effective prayer is routine; that is, looking at prayer as just another thing we must do each day. This type of legalistic mentality blocks us from the exciting and life-giving influence of the Holy Spirit, who is eternal but always new. Routine, or lukewarmness, is like the sepulcher of the spiritual life.

The lukewarm person thinks that he's doing well because he gives time to God every day, but he doesn't really advance in his spiritual life. If we pray just to mark it off our "spiritual checklist," then our prayer is not really a dialogue with God, but with ourselves. Apart from not getting fruit from our prayer, we also run the risk of getting tired and not persevering.

Some people think they are not worthy of prayer. Their reasoning goes like this: "I know that I'm weak in my life, and I don't feel very religious. Prayer is obviously for people who are holier than I am." This is a most insidious temptation, since it ignores the fact that each one of us

Listen closely: It is the hour for your heart.

72

has been created in God's image and likeness, and therefore, that each one of us is by
nature "religious." It is not a question of feelings or attractions; prayer and communication with God is an objective need that all human beings have. It's a great mistake to think
that somehow we were not meant to pray or
communicate with God. That's like saying we
were not meant to breathe or eat, or have a
heartbeat.

Another obstacle, as I stated above, is to
give up on prayer because we don't get results, or we feel arid or dry. We don't go to
prayer to please ourselves or to get a sense
of accomplishment; we go to prayer in order
to please God and to grow in love for him. To
insist that prayer give us the results we want
is really to put shackles on God, to make him
conform to what we want, not what he wants.

It's also true that God may allow us to feel
dry in our prayer so that he can purify us. Often
he will take away our feeling of accomplishment, or the fervor of emotion, so that we can
believe in him and love him in a more unselfish
way. St. Josemaría puts it in this way:

"Your mind is sluggish and won't work. You struggle to coordinate your ideas in the presence of our Lord, but it's useless; a complete fog! Don't force yourself, and don't worry either. Listen closely: it is the hour for your heart" (The Way, no. 102).

This kind of aridity can really be the door to a greater prayer which is close to contemplation. In this highest kind of prayer we don't listen to ourselves any more. Rather, God in his infinite love comes to us in a much deeper way; he is the one who speaks. It was this type of prayer which St. Josemaría himself received from God on more than one occasion.

Some people say that they get easily distracted and therefore cannot pray. But that is the wrong way to look at distractions. Rather than discourage us, they should lead us to pray harder for God's grace and the gift of concentration. Every time we struggle to overcome distractions, we are making an act of faith and love in God. But if the distractions continue, we could consider two approaches:

1. Try to turn them into a dialogue with God: for instance, about our studies,

our family, our temptations and miseries. In this way we can convert a minus into a plus.

2. Keep swatting them away like flies, and use a good book. God will be pleased with our efforts, even if we spend a half-hour swatting away such distractions. God looks at the heart and the will and our continual effort. As Bl. Mother Teresa once said, "God does not want our success, but he does want our sincere struggle."

But the worst of all obstacles to prayer is pride. It's the attitude of someone who thinks that he has everything under control and doesn't really need God's help in his life. Pride is really an exaggerated estimation of ourselves, so that everything in some way must revolve around us: other people, work, entertainment—everything.

In the end, it is a foolish attitude, because the egotistical person places himself in a kind of prison of his own making, with no light or fresh air. He cannot truly know himself or others, let alone the one who made him, and who still loves him despite himself. The Psalmist puts it very succinctly: "The fool says in his heart, 'There is no God'" (Ps 14:1).

This doesn't mean that only atheists or agnostics do not pray or see the need for it. Many people can be "practical atheists" as well. They may believe in God theoretically, and even go to church once a week, but they see no relation between them and him at other times. Literally, they don't want to give him their time or attention because they're too busy with their own projects.

The best answer to all of the above obstacles is knowledge and humility: the knowledge of who we are and who God is, and the humility to pray and ask for his help. If we honestly realize that we do not have such knowledge or humility, now is the moment to work for them and to beg for the grace to receive them.

EXAMPLES OF
PERSONAL PRAYER

The following prayers are only samples of how you can talk with God. Prayer is very personal; it should express what you are really thinking or experiencing, and it should be open to what God wants to tell you. Though the major kinds of prayer are adoration, petition, thanksgiving, and atonement, as we've said above, there are lots of different variations on these four types.

Here are a few. They don't consist of many words, as you can see, but are intentionally short. You can fill in the rest as you do your own mental prayer—or find many other topics of personal communication between you and God as your life goes on, with its good times, tough times, and in-between times. The main thing is to keep praying, and not give up. I wish you all the best.

A Prayer that Strengthens

Lord, I'm pretty tired today. I played basketball all afternoon. I know that I should have left early in order to study. I have a math test tomorrow. But now I just want to check Facebook, or take a nap. Lord, give me the strength to go to my desk and open the book to do my assignment.

I know that you said somewhere that our talents should be used for the good. Now I need your strength to study. I also ask my guardian angel—who is far more intelligent than I am— to help me pass this test. But I need to study. Lord, give me strength.

A Prayer that Forgives

Lord, I'm still angry about that remark that Frank made to me this afternoon. No, I'm not stupid! He just misunderstood my question. As a matter of fact, I get better grades than he does, and I have more friends. What's more, he's the one to blame for…

Wait a minute! I'm not thinking right at this moment. You said, "Forgive your enemies." I'm just holding a grudge right now and even becoming bitter about Frank. I'm way out of line. Give me the grace to forgive, Lord. Tomorrow I'll try to be particularly friendly with Frank, as if nothing happened. It will be hard, but with your help, I'll give it a try.

A Prayer that Consoles

"The Lord is my Shepherd; I shall not want. He leads me through verdant pastures—and though I walk in the valley of the shadow of death, I fear no evil" (Ps 23).

I need to hear these great words, Lord. I feel surrounded by death. There was a murder on campus last night. Everyone is talking about it. The girl lived in the dorms on the north side of campus, and she was in my class. You know that already. A nice girl, though some people say that she was into drugs. O Lord, the truth is that I kind of liked her. What's the sense of it all? If you are good, why did you allow her to be killed?

I know that counselors are coming to talk with us today. But I would prefer for you to talk to me. At times, life does not make any sense. What can I do? Please be my good shepherd, as the psalm says. Take me on your shoulders and comfort me. Tell me that it will be all right. Please, Lord.

A Prayer for More Love

Lord, I just read that the greatest of your commandments is to love. You want us to love you with our whole heart, and soul, and mind, and strength. I must say that it is easier to love a human being—whom I can see and hear— than to love you, God, whom I cannot see. Of course, I believe that you are the Creator of the universe, and that you sustain my every thought, breath, and heartbeat. Really, how could I not love you, and be grateful to you forever? But, Lord, I don't feel that I love you so much, though my mind tells me I should.

Deep down though, Lord, I want to love you above all things. Give me the grace to want it more.

Please help me to see your will, and then give me the courage to carry it out. I'm so weak, Lord: I really cannot love you as you deserve to be loved.

A Prayer that Asks for Forgiveness

Lord, I'm really sorry about last night. I

should have left that party early. People were joking around and drinking too much. I didn't want to appear like a goody-goody, especially when Jack asked me to have another beer. I should have had the strength to say no, to tell him that I had to get up early today, or that I had to study. But he insisted, and I gave in.... I'm sorry that I gave in, Lord, and I am going to get to confession tonight with Fr. Chris.

I do thank you, Lord, for the grace of not going with Liz right afterwards. She also had drunk too much. It would have been so easy for me to take advantage of her. I felt very weak then, so I just left the party and went home. Thanks for that grace, Lord.

And besides going to confession right away, I would like to offer you something more, Lord, to make up for my sin: I'll have no alcohol for a week, including next Saturday night.

A Prayer of Thanksgiving

O Lord, I really don't know how to thank you for this greatest gift of all—your entire self in the Eucharist. And I know that with you I've received all of paradise—your Father, the Holy Spirit, and the angels and saints. And wherever you are, I know that your Mother is very near.

I don't want to receive you out of routine or just sit here watching people in church until the Mass ends. I remember reading what St. Josemaría suggested about thanking you after Communion. Yes, you are my king. We don't live in a monarchy, but I know what a king is, and I would like to serve you today, Lord, in all that I do. You are my teacher. There's so much that I don't understand—things that happen, things that other people do. I especially don't understand myself, and why I never seem to improve. I'm stuck with myself! Teach me, Lord, and heal me. You know my faults well. I am stubborn and angry many times. I'm also lazy. Heal me, Lord; I can't heal myself.

But above all, Lord, I thank you for being my greatest friend. You've come to me in Holy Communion. You never let me down. Sometimes I don't feel your presence during the day, but I know you're there. Even if I were dead, I believe you could raise me up, as you did Lazarus.

And by the way, please help my friend Joe, Lord; he seems to be dead to the Church and to you. Give him life again, Lord.

A Girl's Prayer for Advice

Gina is the prettiest girl in my class, Lord, and she certainly knows it. That's why she has so few real friends, despite all of her parties and boyfriends. I sort of like her though…. She helped me one day with math; she's good at that. But I would like to help her in some way. All the other girls make fun of her behind her back, and most of them won't even talk with her. And we're at a Catholic school, Lord!

What's your advice? I do smile at her once in a while and say hello; I think she appreciates that, though she's never told me so. What if I ask her to play tennis one day, or text her to meet me some place for a talk? I'll say it's an important matter to get her interest. Then, Lord, with your help, I can ask her if she would like to have more friends in our class. She may say no and give me kind of a weird look, but if you give her the grace to say yes, then I can try to suggest a few things. As one girl to another.

And that reminds me, Lord. Please, I don't want her to see me as a holier than thou type… I just want to help her, as you helped so many people when you were on earth.

SOME VALUABLE
VOCAL PRAYERS

Besides the Our Father, Hail Mary, and Glory Be there are many other vocal prayers that can deepen your contact with God, and help you to live in his presence each day.

Morning Offering
(when you wake up in the morning)

O my Jesus, I offer you all my prayers, works, joys, and sufferings of this day in union with your Most Sacred Heart and the Holy Sacrifice of the Mass. Amen.

Act of Faith

O my God, I firmly believe that you are one God in three divine Persons, Father, Son and Holy Spirit; I believe that your divine Son became man and died for our sins, and that he shall come to judge the living and the dead.

I believe these and all the truths that the holy Catholic Church teaches, because you have revealed them, who can neither deceive, nor be deceived.

The Angelus
(which can be said around noon each day)

V. The angel of the Lord declared unto Mary;
R. And she conceived by the Holy Spirit

Hail Mary...

V. Behold the handmaid of the Lord.
R. Be it done unto me according to your word.

Hail Mary...

V. And the Word was made flesh,
R. And dwelt among us.

Hail Mary...

V. Pray for us, O holy Mother of God,
R. That we may be made worthy of the promises of Christ.

Let us pray.

Pour forth, we beseech you, O Lord, your grace into our hearts, that we, to who the incarnation of Christ, your Son, was made known by the message of an angel, may by his passion and cross be brought to the glory of his resurrection, through the same Christ our Lord.

R. Amen.

Psalm 2
(to increase your trust in God)

Ant. His kingdom is a kingdom of all ages, and all kings shall serve and obey him.

1. Why this tumult among nations, among peoples this useless murmuring?
2. They arise, the kings of the earth; princes plot against the Lord and his anointed.
3. "Come, let us break their fetters; come let us cast off their yoke."
4. He who sits in the heavens laughs; the Lord is laughing them to scorn.
5. Then he will speak in his anger, his rage will strike then with terror.
6. "It is I who have set up my king on Zion, my holy mountain."
7. I will announce the decree of the Lord: The Lord said to me: "You are my Son. It is I who have begotten you this day."

8. "Ask and I shall bequeath to you the nations, put the ends of the earth in your possession.

9. "With a rod of iron you will break them, shatter them like a potter's jar."

10. Now, O kings, understand; take warning, rulers of the earth;

11. Serve the Lord with awe and trembling.

12. Pay him your homage, lest he be angry and you perish, for suddenly his anger will blaze. Blessed are they who put their trust in God.

13. Glory be…

Ant. His kingdom is a kingdom of all ages, and all kings shall serve and obey him.

V. O Lord, hear my prayer.

R. And let my cry come unto you.

Let us pray.

Almighty and eternal God, you have renewed all creation in your beloved Son, the king of the whole universe. May all the people of the earth, not torn apart by the wound of sin, become subject to the gentle rule of your only-begotten Son: Who lives and reighns with you and the Holy Spirit, one God, for ever and ever.

R. Amen.

Prayer to St. Michael the Archangel
(to use particularly in time of temptation)

St. Michael the Archangel, defend us in battle. Be our protection against the wickedness and snares of the devil. May God rebuke him, we humbly pray; and do Thou, O Prince of the Heavenly Host—by the Divine Power of God—cast into hell, Satan and all the evil spirits, who roam throughout the world seeking the ruin of souls. Amen.

Inspiring Brief Prayers (Aspirations)
(to be said at any time)

A clean heart create for me, O God (Ps 51:12).

For those who love God, all things work together for good (Rom 3:28).

Here I am, for you did call me (1 Sam 3:5).

I can do all things in him who strengthens me (Phil 4:13).

Not as I will, but as you will (Mt 26:39).

Who can separate us from the love of Christ? (Rom 8:35).

Most Sacred Heart of Jesus, grant us peace.

Mother of fair love, help your children.

Immaculate Heart of Mary, protect me.

YOUR FAVORITE PRAYERS, REFLECTIONS, OR QUOTATIONS

_____

_____

_____

_____

_____

_____

_____

_____

_____

_____

_____

_____

_____

_____